APPLE WATCH SERIES 6

USER GUIDE

Complete User Manual To Master The New Apple Watch Series 6 For Both Beginers And Existing User

Discover New Fertures With This Guide

By

Kelvin L. Wilson

Table of Contents

INTRODUCTION

FERTURES OF APPLE WATCH SERIES 6

watchOS 7 brings new personalization, health, and fitness features to Apple Watch this fall.

Familiarity with sharing watch faces, sleep tracking and automatic hand washing detection

Dance training, Pro Chronograph watch and sleep tracking are featured on the Apple Watch Series 5 separately.

watchOS 7 brings new customization, health and fitness features to the Apple Watch this fall.

Cupertino, CA - Apple today unveiled a preview of watchOS 7, offering enhanced customization tools and powerful new health and fitness features for the world's most advanced smartwatch. Customization is taken to a whole new level with shared and discoverable watch face settings, sleep tracking, automatic handwashing detection, additional types of exercises including dancing, and new mode Hearing health features provide a greater understanding of overall health and are designed with privacy in mind. Comfortable on the wrist, updated maps with bike directions and Siri now offers language translation.

SEE FACE AND SHARE

The face provide customers with valuable information at a glance.. The endlessly customizable faces, including complications, can be shared via messages or mail, and can be discovered through the App Store.

A custom dashboard for shared browsing on iPhone 11 Pro and featured on the Apple Watch Series 5.

You can download custom watch faces from websites.

The app store is shown on the iPhone 11 Pro and is shown on the Apple Watch Series 5.

watchOS 7 offers many ways to discover and share watch faces, including app stores.

watchOS 7 offers interior updates for further customization and access to your favorite apps. The incredibly detailed and accurate Pro Chronograph includes a speedometer based on time elapsed over a fixed distance, Photos' faces offer color filters, and the bold X-Large face now has the option to add a rich complication.

Across a clock, Baby Glow can display multiple complications that help new parents keep track of bottle feeding, breastfeeding, pumping statistics and nap times, while the Dawn Tour can show surfers the tides, wind speed and water temperature of their favorite surf. stain.

The Glow Baby app featured in the Apple Watch 5 series.

New parents can use Glow Baby to see sleep times, changes and meals on one side.

The Dawn Patrol app featured in the Apple Watch 5 series.

Surfers can create a surfing clock with Dawn Peter to track water temperature, inflation and wind speed at their favorite beach.

Nike Run Club complications are featured on the Apple Watch Series 5.

The Nike Run Club can present multiple complications, including the previous running pace and recent achievement.

SLEEP

With watchOS 7, Apple Watch introduces sleep tracking while taking a holistic approach to sleep by providing important tools to help users. You want to sleep the desired amount, go to bed on time and create a bedtime routine to achieve your sleep goals.

Using the micro-motion detection of the accelerometer clock, which indicates breathing during sleep, the Apple Watch cleverly captures when the user is asleep and how much sleep each night. In the morning, the user will see a visualization of the previous night's sleep, including waking periods and sleep. They will also show a graph showing your weekly sleep trend.

The American Academy of Sleep Medicine says, a bedtime routine helps the body prepare for sleep. To support this, Wind Down enable Apple Watch and iPhone users to create a custom bedtime routine. In sleep mode, the Apple Watch automatically turns on Do Not Disturb and darkens the screen at night.

To help users wake up, the Apple Watch offers a quiet silent alarm or soft sounds, while the wake-up screen shows the current battery level. Depending on personal charging behavior, if the battery is low every hour before bed, the Apple Watch will remind users to charge it before bed.

AUTOMATIC HAND WASHING DETECTION

Proper hand washing for at least 20 seconds can help prevent the spread of the disease. In a unique innovation for a wearable device, the Apple Watch uses the device's motion sensors, microphone and machine size to automatically detect movements and hand washingsea. He then starts a 20-second countdown timer, and if the user finishes earlier, he will be asked to continue washing. The Apple Watch can also remind the user to wash their hands when returning home.

After automatic detection, hand washing will begin with a 20-second timer.

TYPES OF EXERCISES AND FITNESS APP

The training app is one of the most popular apps on the Apple Watch, and watchOS 7 offers four exciting new types of exercises backed by powerful custom pulse core training, dance, functional strength training.

To properly capture the caloric effort for Dance, the Apple Watch uses advanced sensor fusion, which combines data from the pulse sensor and accelerometer and gyroscope inputs, which presents the unique challenges in measuring various body-arm movements typical of dance. . This type of training has been verified and tested with four of the most popular dance styles for gymnastics: Bollywood, cardiovascular dance, hip hop and Latin.

The renewed activity app on the iPhone, now called Fitness, provides an efficient view of data that includes daily activity, training, prizes and activity trends in one tab, and joint activity competitions and activity in another.

Activity data is displayed on iPhone 11 Pro and Apple Watch Series 5.

The fitness app on the iPhone has been completely redesigned to provide a more optimal view of your activity data.

LISTENING

After introducing the Noise app on watchOS 6 that measures environmental sound levels and exposure duration, watchOS 7 add additional hearing health support with headphone audio alerts. Customers can now understand how loud they hear media through headphones via iPhone, iPod touch or Apple Watch, and when these levels can affect hearing over time.

When the headphone listening reaches 100 percent of the weekly safe listening volume, a notification will be to the user. This amount is based on the recommendations of the World Health Organization according to which, for example, a person can be exposed to 80 decibels for about 40 hours a week without affecting hearing. How long they were exposed to high decibel levels. Every week in the health app on your iPhone and you can control the maximum level of power of the headphones. The Health app or Apple Watch does not record or save any audio from the headset's audio message format.

watchOS 7 continues to support hearing health through new audio alerts on headphones.

Customers can now use Siri to translate multiple languages conveniently from the wrist, dictation is handled on the device by the power of Apple's edible engine for faster and more reliable processing in dictating messages and more, and the Apple Watch now supports Siri messaging. The shortcuts app is also available on the Apple Watch and can be accessed as a hassle.

Developers can create graphical complications with SwiftUI, and new key tools such as Xcode Preview make creation easier.

BICYCLE TRACK FEATURED IN THE APPLE WATCH

Navigate comfortably by cycling instructions on the Apple Watch.

PRIVACY

Privacy is critical for Apple and is especially important when it comes to health data, so all health features are designed with privacy in mind. Health data is encrypted on a device or iCloud with iCloud syncing, and the data is always under user control

CHAPTER ONE

APPLE HEALTH GUIDE - EXPLAIN A POWERFUL FITNESS APP

How to use Apple Health and some of the best tips to control it

Whether it's walking, cycling, running or even more serious health data like blood pressure and glucose levels, Apple Health can pull data from tracking, smartwatches, scales and other devices and put them in one place.

After its launch in 2014, it has evolved and become a place where even more of this data can live and extract them from devices like the Apple Watch, iPhone, suspension monitors or third-party apps like the Strava. It's more ueful than ever.

Whether you are first introduced to Apple Health or looking for ways to get more out of the software, we discuss how it works, what it can track and more.

WHERE CAN YOU FIND APPLE HEALTH?

The Apple Health app is on the home screen of the iPhone and on the screen of the Apple Watch app if you also have one.

Tap on the white icon with the red heart.

WHAT CAN YOU TRACK IN APPLE HEALTH?

A lot is the simple answer. One thing that needs to be clear about is that Apple Health is unable to track anything on its own. It is about extracting information from the device on which it is installed, applications and compatible third-party devices.

To give you an idea, Apple Health may store data that includes:

- Walking + running distance
- Flights raised
- Heartbeat
- diet
- Sleep surgery
- Heart rate variability

11

- Weight

All of these are listed as health categories in the app browse section.

As you expand these various categories, you will find the most up-to-date data tracked according to the devices and applications that send you data.

In many cases where you are not currently following a particular statistic, Apple recommends apps that work with Health to help you get started.

WHICH APPS WORK WITH APPLE HEALTH?

Along with hardware, it can also extract a variety of data from applications. Go to Apple Health app on your device and scroll down to find apps that work with apple health.

- Water Minder
- Lifesum
- Sleep cycle
- ifertracker
- iHealth My Vitals
- Garmin Connect

- Google fits
- Weight controller
- My Fitness Pal

HOW TO CONNECT AN APPLICATION TO APPLE HEALTH

The way data from those apps is sent to Apple Health will change.

We've detailed how you can connect Strava to Apple Health, for example, to give you an example of what it might look like.

Many applications will offer a notification to share with Apple Health during installation, but you can access the app settings to connect the two if you do not do so immediately.

Once you have granted access, you can go to some of the applications in the health app to see which ones are running.to find the list tap your profile button in the top right corner and tap apps privacy heading.

If you select an application font, it will be accepted in several options.

You can customize the data you want to share with Apple Health or disable the entire service.

On the specific application page in Health, there is also a small data button. If you tap on it, you will be taken to a screen that breaks down the data you obtained from that app. Here you can remove any data that you think is incorrect.

HOW DOES APPLE HEALTH FOLLOW THE STEPS?

If you're interested in tracking, Apple Health does this using the accelerometer's motion sensor inside your iPhone to track traffic. This is the same motion sensor technology used by fitness trackers.

If you use a fitness tracker or smart watch (like the Apple Watch), you can alternatively use these devices to provide your pedometer as long as they are compatible with Apple Health.

It is important to note that Pitbit and Samsung devices do not support Apple Health; However, most of the other mobile devices are.

- Amazfit GTS

- Xiaomi Band 5
- Withings Move ECG
- Garmin Nu

HOW DOES APPLE HEALTH MONITOR SLEEP?

Sleep data is retrieved from Garmin Connect using Fenix 6 to monitor sleep activity.

There are a variety of sleep analysis apps like Sleep ++ and Sleep Cycle that can help improve your sleep insights.

If you want to know which sources send sleep data to Apple Health

Go to summary, then to favorites and then select View all health data

Look for sleep surgery and a matte scroll to find the source of the data and access to it

You'll see a list of data sources that send data to Apple Health

If there are multiple sources, Apple will choose one that will prefer the data displayed

USE APPLE WATCH WITH APPLE HEALTH

you can send data to Apple Health with different devices, Apple Watch can do it perfectly. Not only because it is manufactured by Apple, but also because it can generate a wide range of health and fitness data from the built-in functions and applications of Apple Watch to give you a much more complete picture of your day-to-day (and in some cases, nightly) activities.

Regardless of the Apple watch you have, you can see your VO2 Max, your active energy, your rest energy, your rest hours, your resting heart rate, your average heart rate while walking and your heart rate. Oh, and if you get the breathing reminders from Apple Watch, they will appear in the Mindfulness data in the app.

We have selected some of the best tips for getting the most out of Apple Watch with Apple Health:

VIEW APPLE WATCH DATA IN APPLE HEALTH

You can check all the data directly from your watch by tapping your profile button in the top right corner of the app, tapping devices and selecting your Apple Watch.

You will get a breakdown of all the information that your smartwatch sends to health.

USE THE APPLE WATCH FOR FITNESS TRACKING DATA IN APPLE HEALTH

To ensure that your Apple Watch and not your iPhone provides a step count, there is a simple way to make sure this is the case:

Go to the health app and tap on the profile icon in the top right corner

Select Devices and locate your Apple Watch

Tap Privacy settings and you will see options for turning on / off fitness tracking from your watch

In addition, it offers the same pulse rate and allows the watch to use its microphone to measure ambient levels. It also supports the same audio support from headphones and other audio devices.

SET IRREGULAR PACE ALERTS ON THE APPLE WATCH

One of the newer features utilized is irregular heartbeat alerts. This will allow your Apple Watch, until the end of Series 1, to check for irregular heartbeats. If he recognizes something, he will alert you to see your doctor, as irregular heartbeats can be a sign of atrial fibrillation. If you have a Series 4 or Series 5, all of your ECG calls will also be in the same area.

- Open Apple Health and choose Summary
- Scroll down to find the option to set messages at an irregular rate
- Follow the instructions to complete the alert settings

CHAPTER TWO

THE ECG APP, WHAT IS AN ECG?

An electrocardiogram (also called an ECG or ECG) is a test that records the time and intensity of the electrical signals that cause the heartbeat. By looking at an ECG, a doctor can get information about your heart rate and look for disorders.

HOW TO USE THE ECG APP

The ECG app can record your heart rate and rhythm using the Apple Watch Series 4, Series 5 or Series 6 * electric heart sensor, then check the atrial fibrillation record (AFib), a type of irregular rhythm.

Currently, the ECG app is only available in certain countries and regions.

Make sure the ECG app is available in your country or region.

The ECG application is not intended for use by persons under the age of 22.

INSTALL AND CONFIGURE THE ECG APP

The ECG application is installed during the configuration of the ECG application in the Health application. If you removed the ECG app, you can reinstall it from the app store on your Apple Watch if you have completed the ECG application setup. Follow these steps to configure the ECG application:

- On your iPhone open your health app.
- Follow the steps on the screen. If you do not see a setting message, touch the Browse tab and then touch Heart> Electrocardiograms (ECG)> Set up an ECG application.

After completing the installation, open the ECG app to take ECG.

If you still do not see the app on your Apple Watch, you can search for ECG in the Apple Watch App Store and download it.Take an ECG.

You can take an ECG at any time, when you feel symptoms like a fast or skipping pulse, when you have other general concerns about your heart health

Make sure your Apple Watch is close to your wrist in the Apple Watch app. To check,

- Open the Apple Watch app, tap the 'My Clock' tab and then go to General> Clock Direction.
- Go to ECG app on series 6.
- Place your arms on a table or on your lap.

With your hand in front of your watch, keep your finger on the digital crown. There is no need to click on the digital crown during the session.

The recording lasts 30 seconds. At the end of the recording you will get a rating and then you can tap on Add Symptoms and select your symptoms.

- Touch Save to register any symptoms, then touch Done.

HOW TO READ THE RESULTS

After a successful reading, you will get one of the following results in your ECG application. Regardless of the outcome, if you feel unwell or have any symptoms, you should talk to your doctor.

Atrial fibrillation

The AFib result means that the heart beats in an irregular pattern between 50 and 120 BPM. AF is the most common form of severe arrhythmia or irregular heartbeat.

Low or high pulse

A heart rate lower than 50 BPM and higher than 120 BPM affects the ability of the ECG app to verify AFib, and the recording is considered unequivocal.

The heart rate can be slow because of certain medications or if the electrical signals are not conducted properly through the heart. Learn more about the low heart rate on the American Heart Association.

High heart rate can be due to exercise, stress, irritability, alcohol, dehydration, infection, atrial fibrillation or other arrhythmias. Learn more about high pulse from the American Heart Association.

IF YOU CONSISTENTLY GET AN UNEQUIVOCAL RESULT

If you regularly get an unequivocal result, even after trying the above steps, it could be because of one of the following situations:

Your heart rate ranges from 100 to 120 BPM.

You have a pacemaker or implanted cardio-water defibrillator (ICD).

The recording may show signs of other arrhythmias or heart conditions that the app is not designed to detect.

Certain physiological conditions can prevent a small percentage of users from generating enough signal to produce good recording.

If you need help, contact Apple Support.

VIEW AND SHARE YOUR HEALTH INFORMATION

The shape of the ECG wave, the accompanying classifications and all the specified symptoms will be saved in the health app on your iPhone. You can also share a PDF file with your doctor.

- Open the health app.
- Touch the Browse tab, then touch Heart> Electrocardiograms (ECG).
- Touch the table for your ECG result.
- Tap Export PDF for your doctor.

- Touch the Share button to print or share the PDF.

HOW TO GET THE BEST RESULTS

➢ Place your arms on a table Or in your lap while recording.

➢ Make sure your Apple Watch is not loose on your wrist. The strap should be snug and the back of your Apple Watch should touch your wrist.

➢ Make sure your Apple Watch is on the wrist strap of your Apple Watch app. To check, open the Apple Watch app, tap the 'My Clock' tab and then go to General> Clock Direction.

➢ Stay away from any electronic device connected to an electrical outlet to prevent electrical interference.

A small percentage of people may have certain physiological conditions that prevent them from producing enough signal to produce good documentation; For example, the position of the heart in the chest can change the electrical signal levels, which can affect the ability of the ECG application to achieve measurement.

A fluid-free connection is required for the ECG app to work properly. Use of the ECG application may be affected if the Apple Watch and / or skin are not completely dry. Make sure your wrist and hands are completely dry before attempting to read. To ensure the best reading after swimming, showering, heavy sweating or hand washing, the Apple Watch should be cleaned and dried.

CHAPTER THREE

THE SLEEP APP

APPLE WATCH SLEEP MONITOR: WHAT IT DOES AND HOW TO USE IT

- You can now track your sleep with watchOS 7 update

Why you can count on a lint pocket

(Pocket-lint): In the new watchOS 7 update, Apple lets you track sleep using Apple Watch. We're been testing this on an early (beta) software version for a while now, so here's how to use it along with some ideas on how it works.

WHAT IS SLEEP MONITORING, HOW DOES IT WORK AND WHAT DEVICES OFFER IT

watchOS 7 works with the new Apple Watch Series 3, 4, 5 and Apple Watch Series 6 we are waiting for. It does not match Series 1 or 2.

Sleep tracking was a much sought after feature for the Apple Watch and was previously available in third party apps.

However, there is a sleep app on the clock and it uses motion to detect your sleep time. Obviously you need to use the Apple Watch to keep track of your sleep, so you will need to change its charging behavior and improve the day. If not, it will end free of charge at 10:00 the next morning.

The great thing about Apple Watch sleep tracking is that it is set up and forgotten so that they will monitor your sleep without you having to do anything. But it is completely configurable as you will see.

Apple's sleep tracking is integrated with the sleep feature in the iPhone's Clock app (this feature is now called Sleep), so you can turn it on and create a schedule.

Before the sleep time allotted to you, be 'ready' for sleep with a relaxation time (we set it to 45 minutes here) while your Apple Watch dims and locks; Your watch is currently in sleep mode.

Do not interrupt the power on automatically, but you can turn it off when setting sleep mode on or off.

You can also choose whether you want to receive billing reminders or not - the watch will alert you within an hour before bed if you are charged less than 30 percent.

In sleep mode, you must rotate the digital crown to open the clock, just as you exit the water after swimming.

In fact, we found it a bit annoying when having to get up at night and use a torch, for example. You can disable sleep mode but leave sleep tracking enabled or you can also disable sleep tracking but leave sleep mode on, it's up to you.

Apple's sleep tracking focuses on the amount of time you spend in bed, and as such is less nuanced than some sleep logs like Pitbit's, or excellent jaw tracking if you've used it before. far away. You will know you are not sleeping if you are awake in bed and on your iPhone.

You can access the suspension and tracking options in a number of places, which is a bit confusing at first, but makes sense because it ties some things together. so:

SET UP SLEEP TRACKING ON APPLE WATCH

Make sure your Apple Watch is on watchOS 7 and your iPhone has iOS 14.

➤ In the health app on your iPhone, set sleep. The process can also be performed on the Apple Watch itself in the Sleep app.

➤ First, choose the duration of your sleep - this is the purpose of sleep, but it is not connected to the activity app on the iPhone like your rings (you can see it in the health app on the iPhone). We choose eight hours.

➤ Next, set when to start before bed and when to wake up. There are actually a lot of options here, so check them out carefully. Do you have to set it for every day or just weekdays?

➤ You should set a relaxation time before bed; You can also choose to link it to Siri's shortcut to perform other automation, like turning off a light at home, for example. You can also link Wind Down to a music playlist, for example.

➤ You can decide if you want to set an alarm and how you want it to sound. Note that this will not replace the existing alarms on the Apple Watch (or on your iPhone - you need to turn them off manually).

➤ Your alarm will sound on your iPhone if your Apple Watch is not turned on. You can also set the alarm sound fully. If your watch is silent, it will just vibrate.

➤ You can view your sleep patterns in the iPhone health app: View by week or month. You can win at first I see the gaps in my dream here. As you can see, a young child does not help to reach his dream goal.

CHAPTER FOUR

HOW TO SETUP AND PAIR YOUR IWATCH WITH YOUR IPHONE

You need to make sure your iPhone is running Bluetooth and connected to a Wi-Fi or cellular network.

If you have already set up your Apple Watch but would like to use it with another iPhone, you can transfer your Apple Watch and its contents to your new iPhone.

➤ Turn on your Apple Watch and turn it on
➤ Side button on Apple Watch.

Wait for the message, then tap Continue. If you do not see this message, open the Apple Watch app and then tap Start Adjusting.

Keep the Apple Watch and iPhone together until you complete the following steps.

➤ Hold your iPhone over the animation

Center the dashboard in your iPhone viewfinder. Wait for the notification that your Apple Watch is optimized.

If you can not use the camera, tap the Apple Watch manually and then follow the steps below. Learn what to do if you do not see the "I" icon.

- ➢ Set as new or restored from backup
- ➢ Sign in with your Apple ID

Some features that require a mobile phone number will not work on Apple Watch mobile models unless you sign in. To iCloud.

If Find My is not set on your iPhone, you will be prompted to activate the activation lock. If you see an activation lock screen, your Apple Watch is already linked to the Apple ID. You must enter the email address and password for this Apple ID to continue the installation. If your Apple Watch was previously owned, you may need to contact the previous owner to unlock the activation.

- ➢ Choose your configuration

Your Apple Watch shows you what settings it shares with your iPhone. If you turn on Find My, location services, Wi-Fi, and diagnostics for your iPhone, those settings are automatically turned on for your Apple Watch.

You can choose to use other settings, such as track tracking and pots. If Siri is not yet set up on your iPhone, it will turn on after you select this option.

> ➤ Create a password

You can skip creating a password code, but you need code for features like Apple Pay.

On your iPhone, tap Create Password or Add Long Password, then go to your Apple Watch to enter your new password. To skip, tap Do not add password.

You will also be asked to set up Apple Pay by adding a card.

> ➤ Select features and apps

We will guide you in defining features like SOS and activity. With mobile Apple Watch models, you can set up mobile data.

Then you can install your Apple Watch compatible apps.

> ➤ Wait for your devices to sync

Depending on the amount of data you have, synchronization may take some time. While you wait for your watch to sync, try the basics of the Apple Watch to learn a little about how to wear your watch.

Hold your devices together until you hear a bell and feel a gentle touch from your Apple Watch, then push the digital crown.

➤ Start using your Apple Watch

Learn about the gestures that control your Apple Watch and the apps you can use. You can also read the Apple Watch User Guide, customize your dashboard, or add or remove apps.

If you need help, contact Apple Support.

If you are prompted for a password

Your Apple Watch is still compatible with another iPhone. If you do not remember the access code, you must delete the Apple Watch and set it again.

If you see an activation lock screen

Your Apple Watch is fitted with an Apple ID. You must enter the email address and password for this Apple ID to continue the installation. If your Apple Watch was previously owned, you may need to contact the previous owner to unlock the activation.

If you are unable to set up your Apple Watch or have received an error message

Your iPhone must run the latest version of iOS.

Switch your iPhone off and turn it on again.

Turn off the Apple Watch and turn it on again.

CHAPTER FIVE

MASTER THE IWATCH SCREEN ICONS

Status icons and icons on the Apple Watch

Green thunder

➢ Your Apple Watch is charging.

➢ Your battery is low.

> Airplane enable

Flight mode is on. Wireless features are disabled until you disable this setting. You can still use other functions on your watch. When you turn off Flight Mode on your watch, Flight Mode remains active on your iPhone.

Moon symbol

Theater status icon

Theater mode or theater mode are turned on. Quiet mode also works, and the screen stays dark until you touch it, press a button or rotate the digital crown. This mode also darkens the dark screen even when using the Always On feature. To disable theater mode, open the Control Center and tap the icon.

Green dots symbol

Apple Watch is not connected to your iPhone. Bring your devices closer together or turn off the plane.

Red x symbol

Your Apple Watch with GPS + Cellular has lost its connection to the cellular network.

Water drop symbol

The water lock is on and the screen does not respond to touches. Rotate the digital crown to unlock your Apple Watch. The water drop icon only appears on the Apple Watch Series 2 or later and on the Apple Watch SE. Apple Watch Series 1 and Apple Watch (Generation 1) are not suitable for swimming. Learn more about water resistance in your Apple Watch.

Red dot symbol

You have received a message. Slide down on the dashboard to read it.

Bluetooth icon

Press the audio button to switch the audio output between Bluetooth headsets, speakers and custom accessories.

Arrow symbol

Application in your Apple Watch Use location services.

Lock icon

Your Apple Watch is locked. Touch to enter the access code.

Icon before bed

Your Apple Watch is in sleep mode. To exit sleep mode, slide to the control center and tap the sleep icon.

Active application icons

With watchOS 5 or later, your Apple Watch displays active apps, such as the walkie-talkie or phone app icon, at the top of the dashboard. Touch the icon to open the application. For example, if you receive instructions from the Maps icon, the icon will appear at the top of the screen.

It appears when you use training. If you still see the training icon after training, please reset your watch.

Tap to open the walkie-talkie, where you can connect with friends instantly.

Now an icon game

While the audio is playing, the Now Playing icon appears at the top of the screen.

It appears when browsing through a third-party application. If you still see the navigation icon after completing the navigation, please reset the clock.

With watchOS 7, the microphone icon says the microphone on your Apple Watch is listening.

CHAPTER SIX

UNPAIR AND DELETE YOUR APPLE WATCH

Unapproaching the Apple Watch returns it to its factory settings.

HOW TO UNMATCH YOUR APPLE WATCH FROM YOUR IPHONE

Keep Apple Watch and iPhone together while unplugging.

- Go to your Watch app in your iPhone.
- Go to the My Clock tab and tap on all clocks.
- Tap the info button next to the clock you want to cancel the match.
- Tap Cancel Apple Watch Pair.

HOW TO DELETE YOUR APPLE WATCH IF YOU DO NOT HAVE YOUR IPHONE

On your Apple Watch.

- Tap Settings, then General and tap Reset to Delete all content including settings.
- Enter your password if prompted.

CHAPTER SEVEN

ADJUST THE BRIGHTNESS, TEXT SIZE, SOUNDS AND OPTICS OF THE APPLE WATCH

Brightness settings on the Apple Watch, with the brightness indicator at the top and the Always On button below.

- Open the Settings app on your Apple Watch, then tap View and Brightness to adjust the following:
- Brightness: Touch the brightness controls to adjust, or touch the slider and then rotate the digital crown.
- Text Size: Tap Text Size then tap the letters or rotate the digital crown.
- Bold text: Play bold text.

HOW TO MUTE THE RINGTONE AND ALERTS ON YOUR APPLE WATCH

Sometimes it is necessary to mute your Apple Watch for any situation or peace of mind.

Whether you are in the midst of a romantic dinner or you need a quiet moment, from time to time it is wise to mute the Apple Watch through quiet mode. This is a fairly simple process as you can see here.

Some things to remember always.

On the Apple Watch, quiet and uninterrupted mode is not the same. With the first one, only the sound is muted, which means the patics will still play it as needed.

Also, silent mode does not silence Apple Watch alarms or timers.

Use silent mode on your Apple Watch

- Click on the digital crown to make sure it is on the surface of the Apple Watch.

- Move up so you can see the control center.

- Scroll down and press the mute button, which has a bell icon.
- Scroll up on the clock, press the mute button marked with a bell icon

You can also mute your Apple Watch from the Watch app on the iPhone:

In the Clock app on the My Clock tab, tap Sound & Taps.

At the top of the screen, turn on silent mode.

Follow the steps above to turn off the Apple Watch mute.

Other mute solutions for Apple Watch

Quiet mode is not the only Apple Watch feature that mutes sounds. There is also a theater mode, which is almost identical to a silent mode, except that the Apple Watch screen does not light up at a glance, and do not disturb, which turns off sounds and taps in the wearable device.

CHAPTER EIGHT

HOW TO ACTIVATE DO NOT DISTURB

Unlike mute, do not disturb turning off sounds and taps on your Apple Watch.

A dark watch worn on the wrist shows the control center open and not activated.

Do Not Disturb work is to collect alerts without knowing you. It may sound strange, but if you are sleeping, in a meeting, at the movies, or in a place where you do not want noise or caregivers to bother you, but you do not want a list of everything you have. In the meantime, do not disturb is exactly what you need.

HOW TO CONFIGURE DO NOT DISTURB WITH THE APPLE WATCH

- Open the Apple Watch app on your iphine Scroll down and tap Rules.
- Touch Do Not Disturb.
- Turn on iPhone mirror.

You can also automatically turn on Do Not Disturb when you start training by running Do Not Disturb workout.

HOW TO MANUALLY ACTIVATE DO NOT DISTURB YOUR APPLE WATCH

- Push the digital crown all the way down to your watch.
- Slide up to open the Control Center.
- Touch the Do Not Disturb button.
- From the list that appears, select the length of time Do Not Disturb.

CHAPTER NINE

MANAGE MAIL ON APPLE WATCH

Choose which mailboxes appear on the Apple Watch

- Go to Apple Watch app on your iPhone.
- Touch my watch and then go to Mail> Include Mail.
- Choose the accounts you will like to see on your Apple Watch. You can specify multiple accounts, such as iCloud and the account you use at work.

If you want, touch the account and then touch specific mailboxes to view their contents on your Apple Watch.

By default, you see messages from all your inboxes. You can also choose to view VIP messages, marked messages, unread messages and more.

You can also select the accounts and mailboxes you see, directly in the Apple Watch. Open the Mail app, scroll down, tap Edit, and then tap Account or Mailbox.

VIEW SPECIFIC APPLE WATCH ACCOUNTS

- Launch the Mail app in your Apple Watch.

- Touch <in the upper right corner to see a list of special accounts and mailboxes, such as marked and unread.
- Touch an account or mailbox to view its contents.

DELETE, MARK UNREAD OR READ, OR MARK A MESSAGE

- Open the Mail app on your Apple Watch, open an email, and scroll to the bottom:
- Delete message: Tap Trash.

If you are looking at the message list, swipe left on the message and then click the trash button.

Mark unread or unread message: Tap "Mark unread" or "Mark unread."

If you are looking at the message list, swipe right above the message and then click the Read or Read button.

CUSTOMIZE ALERTS

- Go to apple watch app in your iphone.
- Touch My Clock, go to Mail> Custom, touch Account and then turn on View Alerts from [Account Name].

59

- Turn on or disable sound and apathy.

SHORTEN YOUR MESSAGE LIST

To make the mailing list more compact, reduce the number of lines of preview text displayed for each email in the list.

- on your iPhone open the apple watch app.
- Touch my watch, touch the mail and then touch the preview message.
- Choose to display only one or two rows, or none of them.

UPLOAD REMOTE IMAGES

Some emails may contain links that point to images online. If you are allowed to upload remote images, those images will appear in the email. To enable these images, follow these steps:

- Launch the Apple Watch app in your iPhone.
- Touch my watch, touch email, touch custom and turn on uploading remote images.

Note: Uploading remote photos may slow down email downloads on your Apple Watch.

ARRANGE BY THREAD

To see all email responses combined in one thread, follow these steps:

- Go to your iPhone and open the apple watch app.
- Touch my watch, touch mail, touch custom and run organization by thread.

CHAPTER TEN

MANAGE PHONE CALLS ON YOUR APPLE WATCH

Although you can't even use your iPhone as a phone, did you know that you can use your watch as a phone? If you have an Apple Watch, you can do just that, make and answer calls right from your wrist.

You can call without taking your phone out of your pocket thanks to your Apple Watch.

Use this guide to get started with your Apple Watch.

HOW TO MAKE A PHONE CALL WITH SIRI ON APPLE WATCH

The fastest way to start a phone call from your Apple Watch is to call Siri.

❖ Say hi to Siri or click and hold the digital crown on your Apple Watch to turn Siri on.

❖ Tell Siri who you want to call (example: "Call Joe").

❖ Say hi Siri, say the name of the person you want to call

❖ Touch the number you want to call, if there is more than one option.

62

HOW TO MAKE A PHONE CALL FROM THE APPLE WATCH PHONE APP

Of course, you can also use the built-in phone app to scroll through your favorite, recent or even your entire contact list.

- Open the phone app from your Apple Watch home screen.
- Touch Favorites, Recently, Contacts or Keyboards
- Touch the name or number of the contact you want to call, or dial the number manually if you are using the keypad
- Touch the green button on the phone to call if you are using the keypad.
- Tap on the name, then the green button

ANSWER PHONE CALL ON YOUR APPLE WATCH

When you receive a call, you can leave your phone in your pocket and answer it with one touch.

- Raise your wrist or touch the screen to see your incoming call.

- Touch the green answer button.

- Press the mute button if you need to mute a call.

- Tap Reply, tap Mute

- Rotate the digital crown to change the volume of the call.

- Press the red hang button when you end the call.

- Rotate the crown to change the volume, touch Drop to end the call

HOW TO SEND A MISSING MESSAGE INSTEAD OF ANSWERING A CALL

Just like you can on an iPhone, you can use your Apple Watch to send a pre-made text message to a caller if you are unable to talk to them at this time.

- When a call comes in Tap on the button.

- Tap one of the predefined messages if you cannot talk to the person right away.

CHAPTER ELEVEN

HOW TO TRANSFER A CALL, MESSAGE OR A EMIL FROM APPLE WATCH TO IPHONE

The Apple Watch is great for quick responses, but if you need more conversation, your iPhone is here to rescue you.

HOW TO TRANSFER A CALL FROM APPLE WATCH TO IPHONE

If the call keeps ringing on your Apple Watch, use the digital crown to scroll down until you see the Answer button on iPhone. Tap it and your recipient will be on hold until you can pick up your iPhone. (There's even a Ping button to find your iPhone if you're not sure where it is in the house.

Apple Watch call iPhone

If you have already answered the call on your Apple Watch, you can transfer it to your iPhone in one of two ways:

- If your iPhone is locked, tap on the phone icon in the upper left corner of the screen.
- If your iPhone is unlocked, tap the time at the top of the screen.

TRANSFER MESSAGE FROM APPLE WATCH TO IPHONE

- Open the messages app on your apple watch.
- Touch the thread in question that you want to reply to. open the message t on your iPhone.

TRANSFER MESSAGES TO IPHONE

- Select the app switcher on your iOS device.
- Touch the Handoff option; appears as a banner under applications.

HOW TO TRANSFER EMAIL FROM APPLE WATCH TO IPHONE

- Open the Mail app on your Apple Watch.
- Touch the thread in question that you want to view or reply to. You can then open the message thread on your iPhone.

CHAPTER TWELVE

HOW TO LISTEN TO VOICE MESSAGE ON APPLE WATCH

If your iPhone is not nearby and you receive a voice message, you can listen to it directly on your Apple Watch.

The Apple Watch allows us to worry less about where our iPhones are, especially when we do things at home or in the office. If you get an important voicemail, you will not have to wait until you get back to your iPhone to hear it. Instead, you can use the phone app directly on your Apple Watch.

- in your Apple Watch open the phone app
- Touch voicemail.
- Then select the voicemail you want.

CHAPTER THIRTEEN

CHECKING YOUR CALENDAR ON APPLE WATCH WITH SIRI

Lift your Apple Watch here and say "Hello Siri", or press and hold the digital crown to activate Siri.

Ask Siri about the calendar information you want to know, or just say something like "Show me my diary."

"How's my schedule tomorrow?"

"What events do I have today?"

Ask Siri what diary information you want to see

It is important to note that your Apple Watch diary will be released only 7 days in advance. So if you ask Remover to give you information on anything more than seven days from now (or even in the past), it will not be available.

HOW TO CHECK THE CALENDAR ON APPLE WATCH USING THE APP

- Click the digital crown on the Apple Watch to go to your home screen.
- Find the log app icon and click to launch it.

- Click Digital Crown to display the home screen, find the calendar icon and tap it to activate
- Touch the desired view.
- In list view or day, you can touch> today to go to month view.
- Press firmly to bring up the views, touch the desired view, touch> Today to return to the month

HOW TO RESPOND TO CALENDAR ORDERS ON YOUR APPLE WATCH

If you receive an event invitation on your calendar, you can reply directly to your Apple Watch instead of your iPhone.

- When you see the order as soon as it arrives: Scroll to the bottom of the message and tap Accept, maybe or reject.
- If you see the message later: Tap the invitation in your messages, scroll down and reply.
- If you're already on the calendar app: Tap the event to reply.

HOW TO USE THE CALENDAR APP ON YOUR APPLE WATCH

Your Apple Watch lets you check your schedule directly on your wrist!

We all have very busy schedules during our day to day life. This is why keeping a digital diary is the best way to keep track of everything you need to do and what to go through throughout the day. You can see your schedules without bringing your iphone out of your pocket. Here you will find everything you need to know about using the calendar app on your Apple Watch.

follow these steps:

- Click the digital crown button to go to the home screen.
- Touch Apply Calendar.

This triggers the calendar application. By default, you should see the current view of the day, with your upcoming events in chronological order.

Use the finger pad to scroll down to view future dates or rotate the digital crown knob toward you.

This experience is similar to the calendar app on the iPhone. The current time also appears in the upper right corner of the calendar application.

CHAPTER FOURTEEN

TRACKING YOUR WORKOUTS AND ACTIVITIES ON APPLE WATCH

The Apple Watch has always been a useful tool for tracking and recording workouts and exercise, but you can do even more with watchOS 6.

The new version gives you the option to add a variety of different workouts and activities to keep track of. And with the activity app on your iPhone, you can view your training progress and find tips for improving your fitness.

START TRAINING

When you are ready to track a workout or activity, open the workout app on your watch. Divide between the various activities until you find the desired action, such as indoor cycling, indoor cycling, elliptical, outdoor track or stairs.

CONDUCT TRAINING

If you want to set the workout to a specific number of calories, distance, time or other factor, tap the ellipse icon () in the workout and select the desired option. Otherwise, tap the workout to begin.

Pause your workout at any time by swiping the screen to the right and pressing the pause button. When done, swipe right and tap Finish. A summary screen shows your total time, calories and other data. Scroll to the bottom of the summary screen and tap Done to record your workout.

ADD TRAINING

Apple Watch offers a number of default workouts; Trips and yoga were added to the mix in 2018. However, if you do not see the desired workout, you can choose from a variety of additional activities added with watchOS 6.

To do this, scroll to the bottom of the training list and select Add Training. Frist its list out pupolar workout, Swipe down on the screen to watch a variety of other activities and sports, arranged alphabetically, including archery, bowling, horseback riding, golf, hockey, jumping rope, rowing, tai chi, wrestling and more.

TRAINING REMINDERS

You can set reminders on your Apple Watch to instruct you to start and stop training if the watch detects that you are engaging in any type of exercise. This option is enabled automatically on watchOS 5 and watchOS 6, but can be disabled.

Go to Settings, scroll down and tap Workout. Swipe down the workout screen to see the workout reminder options and workout end reminders; Turn off one or both reminders by touching the switch.

The only downside is that it can take a few minutes for the training reminder to notice that you are training and even longer to realize that you have stopped. Therefore, this function is best suited for longer workouts, such as a long walk or a bike ride.

RECORD WORKOUTS

If reminders are turned on and you are in the middle of a workout, your watch should ask if you want to record it. Start walking, running or cycling without telling your watch. If it notices, it should identify the activity you are doing and ask if you want to record it.

The request appears as a message on your watch and offers several options: recording training, changing training, day silence and closing. You can choose to record the workout if the watch detects the correct activity. The device will also ask you to stop recording after you have determined that you have finished training.

TRAINING SETTINGS

In the settings training screen, you can enable or disable other options. Power save mode turns off cellular connectivity and the built-in pulse sensor during walking / running training to extend battery life.

Enable auto-pause pause to automatically pause workouts when you stop moving and resume them when you start moving again. Enable gym equipment locator to synchronize your workouts with compatible fitness equipment.

WATCH ACTIVITY ON APPLE WATCH

Once you have collected some workouts, you can check your workouts history through the activity app on your watch. The app displays your current activity in the form of rings around the circle and individual charts.

The red Move graph shows the calories you burned from the beginning of the day. The green exercise graph indicates how much time you have invested in exercise so far. And the blue class graph indicates the number of hours you spent standing in that day.

VIEW ACTIVITY HISTORY

The activity app on your iPhone offers much more data and options than the clock version. Open the activity app on your phone. The History tab shows activity data and details for the current day. Touch the left arrow next to the month at the top of the screen to view a calendar. You can then select a specific date to view the information for that day.

SEE ACTIVITY TRENDS

The new activity app, courtesy of watchOS 6, is the Trends tab. Here you can check your daily training and activity trends to see how many calories you burn, how long you exercise, how long you stand and how far you travel. The Trends section also provides tips on how to improve results for a specific goal. Touch each item to see more details about it.

VIEW TRAINING HISTORY

The training tab in the activity app shows your training activity per month

Tap the All Workouts link at the top and you can filter the list to see only specific workouts.

SHARE ACTIVITY DATA

You can challenge a friend to bring an Apple Watch to a fitness competition to cheer you both up. To get started, you must first share your activity data with your friend. Touch the share icon and touch at the beginning of the work. Press the + button and select the person you want from your contact list.

Touch Send to send the invitation to your friend.

Once the person agrees, their name appears on the sharing screen.

UPDATE YOUR HEIGHT AND WEIGHT

- In your iPhone you're the apple watch app.
- Touch my watch, go to Health> Health Details, then touch Edit.
- Touch height or weight then adjust.

Your Apple Watch uses information you provide about your height, weight, mech, age and wheelchair to calculate how many calories you burn, how far you travel and other information. The more you run with the workout app, the more your Apple Watch learns about your fitness level and can more accurately estimate the calories you burned during aerobic exercise.

Your iPhone's GPS allows your Apple Watch to achieve even greater distance accuracy. For example, if you carry your iPhone while using the training app while running, your Apple Watch uses the iPhone's GPS to gauge your pace. The Apple Watch can use the built-in GPS to calibrate its movement.

CHANGE YOUR TRAINING VIEW

- In your iphone go and open the apple watch app.
- Touch My Watch, go to Tutorial> Training View and then touch Multiple Value or Single Meter.
- Multiple Index shows you multiple statistics on a single screen.

To select which statistics will be displayed for each type of training, for example if you want to see your current altitude while hiking in the mountains, tap the type of training, tap Edit, then add or remove statistics and drag to rearrange.

During training, rotate the digital crown to emphasize another measure - distance or pulse, for example.

CHANGE UNITS OF MEASURE

If you prefer meters over meters or pounds over calories, you can change the units of measure used by the training app.

- On your apple watch open the setting app
- Touch the workout, scroll to the bottom and then touch the units of measure.

You can change the energy units, pool length, bike training, and walking and running training.

- Pause running training automatically
- Go to Settings app.
- Tap Workout and then turn on Auto Run Stop.

Your Apple Watch will automatically stop your outdoor workout.

ENABLE OR DISABLE TRAINING REMINDERS

For many workouts, your Apple Watch detects when you move and warns you to launch the workout app. It even gives you credit for the exercise you have already performed. It will also remind you to finish the workout, in case you are distracted when it cools down. Follow these steps to turn the exercise reminders on or off.

- On your apple watch go to setting.
- Touch a workout, then change the settings for a workout reminder and a workout reminder. (Training reminders are turned on by default.)

AVOID TOUCHING ACCIDENTALLY

If the exercise you are doing or the equipment you are using is causing accidental difficulty in your Apple Watch,

- Lock the screen so that your training log is not disturbed.
- Lock the screen: slide right and tap lock.
- Reject message: click on the digital crown.
- Screen lock: rotate the digital crown.

SAVE ENERGY DURING TRAINING

You can extend the battery life of your Apple Watch during walking and running training.

- Go to Settings.
- Touch the workout and then turn on the power save mode.

During walking and running training, the power save mode disables the Always On display and the cell phone in models that support these features. The built-in pulse sensor also shuts off until you finish training.

END, PAUSE OR LOCK THE WORKOUT

❖ To finish the workout, slide your finger to the right and then press the end button or the X button.

❖ To pause a workout, swipe right and press the Pause button or the Pause button. Alternatively, you can press the digital crown and the side button at the same time. To continue, press the two buttons again.

❖ To lock the screen and avoid accidental touching, swipe right and then press the lock button. To open the screen, rotate the digital crown. Learn to pause or finish a swimming workout.

CHAPTER FIFTEEN

HOW TO SWITCH WRISTS OR CHANGE THE DIGITAL CROWN ORIENTATION ON IWATCH

Set the direction of the wrist and crown on your Apple Watch

- Raise your hand to hold your apple watch.
- click Digital Crown.
- From the Home screen, tap Settings.
- tap General.
- touch the direction you want.
- In the wrist area of the direction screen, tap left or right, as needed.
- Now rotate the digital crown clockwise to scroll down.
- In the crown area, touch left or right, whichever you prefer.
- Touch the direction again and the general screen will appear.

CHAPTER SIXTEEN

CHARGE THE APPLE WATCH

Set the charger

- Connect to power adapter and plug it into a wall socket.
- Start charging your Apple Watch
- Insert the magnetic charging cable into the back of the Apple Watch. The concave end of the charging cable fits magnetically into the back of your Apple Watch and aligns it properly.

You can charge your Apple Watch in flat mode with the band open or on its side.

If you use the Apple Watch Magnetic Charging Station: Place your Apple Watch on the dock.

CHECK THE REMAINING POWER

To see the remaining power, touch and hold the bottom of the screen and then swipe up to open the control center. To more quickly test the remaining power, add a battery complication to the face of the watch. See Customizing the Clock Panel.

The clock face shows the complication in the battery percentage in the upper right corner.

SAVE POWER WHEN THE BATTERY IS LOW

To do this follow this easy steps:

- Press and hold the bottom of the screen and then slide up to open the control center.
- Tap the battery percentage, then drag the reserved power slider to the right.
- The Power Reserve screen displays the end button in the upper right corner, the percentage of battery remaining, and the Power Reserve indicator.

Tip: If you have battery-powered devices, such as AirPods, that are connected to your Apple Watch via Bluetooth, the billing balance appears on this screen.

When the battery drops to 10 percent or less, your Apple Watch alerts you and gives you the option to enter Power Reserve mode.

Low power alert includes a button that can be pressed to enter power standby mode.

When your Apple Watch is low on power, it automatically switches to power save mode.

Tip: For tips on how to maximize battery life, see Maximizing Battery Life and Battery Life on the Apple website.

CHECK THE BATTERY STATUS

You can find out the battery capacity of your Apple Watch relative to a new situation.

- Go to setting
- Touch the battery and then touch the battery status.

To reduce battery aging, the Apple Watch learns from your workout routine. Charged daily so you can wait until it's over 80 percent charged before you need to use it.

The Apple Watch alerts you if your battery capacity drops significantly, allowing you to verify your service options.

CHAPTER SEVENTEEN

ORGANIZE APPS ON APPLE WATCH

Rearrange your applications in the network view

> - On your Apple Watch, click on the digital crown to go to the home screen.
> - If the screen is in list view, open the settings app on your Apple Watch, tap app view, then tap network view.
> - Click Digital Crown, click and hold an app until it moves, then drag it to a new location.
> - Apple Watch home screen in network view.
> - Click on the digital crown when done.

Or open the Apple Watch app on your iPhone, tap my watch, tap app view, and then tap deployment. Long press on the app icon and then drag it to a new location.

Note: In the list view, the applications are always arranged in alphabetical order.

The arrangement screen in the Apple Watch app that displays a network of icons.

Remove app from Apple Watch

Web View: From the Home screen, touch and hold the app icon until you see an X in the icon, then tap the X to remove the app from your Apple Watch. It stays in your custom iPhone, unless you delete it there as well.

List View: Slide the app to the left and then tap the Trash button to remove it from your Apple Watch. It stays in your custom iPhone, unless you delete it there as well.

CHECK THE STORAGE USED BY APPLICATIONS ON APPLE WATCH

➢ Go toSettings.
➢ Go to General> Usage.

INSTALL APPS ON YOUR APPLE WATCH

➢ Click on the digital crown to display the home screen and then touch the App Store.
➢ Touch the search to find apps using Scribble or Dictation, or scroll down to discover top apps and collections of selected apps.
➢ Touch the app to see its description, ratings and reviews, screenshots, version comments and more.
➢ Tap the price or tap Accept.

➤ When prompted, double-click the side button to download and install the application.

When you download an app you have not previously downloaded to your watch, it automatically appears on your iPhone. To manage this, open the Settings app on your iPhone, then tap iTunes and the App Store. Under Automatic Downloads, Launch or Disable Applications.

HOW TO REMOVE APPS FROM HOME SCREEN

Click on the digital crown to display the home screen.

If your home screen is in web view, touch and hold the app until the app icons move. If the apps do not move, make sure you do not press too hard. Tap the delete button in the app you want to delete, then tap Delete app.

If your home screen is in list view, swipe left in the app you want to delete and then tap the red delete button.

Click on the digital crown to finish.

If you delete a built-in Apple app from your iPhone, the app will also be removed from your Apple Watch.

Update your Apple Watch apps

Enable automatic downloads and updates, or check for app updates manually.

HOW TO KEEP APPS ON YOUR APPLE WATCH AUTOMATICALLY UPDATED

- Click on the digital crown to display the home screen and then touch the settings.
- Touch the app store.
- Enable automatic downloads to automatically download new app purchases you make on other devices. Enable automatic updates to automatically download new versions of your applications.

HOW TO CHECK FOR UPDATES TO APPLE WATCH MANUALLY

- Go to apple store and scroll down.
- Touch the account.
- Touch Updates.
- Touch Update next to an application to update only that application, or touch Update all.

HOW TO ALWAYS DISPLAY THE LAST USED APP ON THE APPLE WATCH

You can do this through your iphone.

- Go to setting
- Slide down and tap Rules
- Slide down again and tap the wake-up screen and complete it.

You are now arranged so that the last app used is the default when you lift the wrist.

REARRANGE THE HOME SCREEN APP ICONS

Here's how to rearrange the icons directly on the Apple Watch:

➢ On the Apple Watch home screen, press and hold until the application icons start moving, just like when you move icons on the home screen of your iPhone.

➢ Then just drag the apps to new locations.

➢ When you are done, click on the digital crown.

HIDE APPS ON APPLE WATCH

To make the home screen usable, it may be best to hide certain apps. Again, this can be done on an Apple Watch or iPhone.

> ➢ To hide app icons directly on the Apple Watch:
> ➢ Go to the Apple Watch home screen by clicking on the digital crown.
> ➢ Click and hold the application icons until they move; A small X will appear to the left of the apps that can be removed, tap it.

Note: None of the pre-installed apps like Watch, Photos and Passbook can be uninstalled. Also, the apps hidden on the watch remain installed on your iPhone, unless you delete them there as well.

CHAPTER EIGHTEEN

HOW TO CONFIGURE AND USE APPLE WATCH ACTIVITY SHARING

How do I set up and share activities on my Apple Watch? You will need to invite people to use your iPhone.

If you want to train with friends or find a healthy competition between you and another important person to achieve your fitness goals, the Activity app can help.

WHAT ACTIVITY DATA ARE SHARED WHEN I CONNECT WITH FRIENDS?

When you add a friend to your sharing screen, you will see all of his activity data from that day on, and they will also receive all of yours. But what exactly are activity data? It is divided into several categories:

Your day's activities ring (movement, exercise and standing) and your personal goals for each one

- Calories burned
- Protocol Protocol
- The hours stopped
- Steps taken
- Driving distance

Your Apple Watch and Activity app will never share with your friends more personal and confidential data, such as your heartbeat or any other health data that the watch may collect.

You also will not get a full date view of your friends' data in the same way that you can browse yours. You will have activity data for a week on the sharing screen and you can tap on your friend's profile for each of those single days, but you will not be able to see a graph of their movement over time or any major trend lines. information.

HOW TO ENABLE ACTIVITY SHARING

To enable activity sharing with your friends, you will need to use your iPhone and the activity app. If you try to do this directly from the Apple Watch, you will see a message that says, "To start sharing your activity, use the activity app on your iPhone."

- Open the activity app from your iPhone's.
- Touch the Share button.
- A red plus sign will show click on it.

- Enter the name or Apple ID of the friend with whom you would like to share your activity progress.
- Click Submit.

Write the name of the friend and tap Send in the right corner of the dinner

Once you're done, you can see your progress with your friends in the activity app's sharing pane.

HOW TO SHARE YOUR ACTIVITY RINGS WITHOUT USING THE ACTIVITY SHARING FEATURE

Want to show off to someone who doesn't have an Apple Watch? You can share your activity rings as a separate image from the sharing screen. This is how.

- From the sharing screen, touch Me.
- Tap the Share button.
- Touch Save image, copy, message, email, or any other sheet sharing option.

HOW TO SEE YOUR FRIENDS' SHARED ACTIVITY DATA

After adding some friends to your sharing screen, you will see their activity rings appear along with their name and (by default) the percentage of their movement goals and calories burned.

If you do not like calories and are more interested in exercise or mileage, you can touch the text in the upper left corner to change the metrics: you can sort by alphabetical name, purpose of movement, purpose of exercise, steps or number of workouts.

View author data on Apple Watch

You can also send your friends a joke or exercise-related gif by tapping the message button in the top right corner. It is not yet possible to create activity groups, though you can send messages to people individually.

Bulk notification from the activity app

HOW TO VIEW, MUTE AND DELETE THE ACTIVITY DATA OF A SPECIFIC MEMBER ON YOUR IPHONE

- Tap the person from the sharing list to view their activity profile. It shows your movement rings, calorie burning, exercise data, support rings, steps and distance for the day.

- To mute alerts about this person's activity, tap Mute alerts.

To send them an encouraging text message (or several calls), tap the message button in the upper right corner.

To view your contact card, tap the info button in the upper right corner.

HIDE YOUR ACTIVITY DATA FROM FRIENDS

Have you been embarrassed by your recent activity data? Are you going on vacation and do not want your friends to know how many steps you are not taking? You can hide your activity data by a friend in a few quick steps.

- Visit your friend's activity profile.

- Scroll down and tap Hide My Activity. All your data activity will be hidden until further notice.
- To run Share again, just tap Stop hiding my activity.

CHAPTER NINETEEN

SET UP SIRI ON APPLE WATCH

Siri on Apple Watch is essentially linked to your iPhone - if you have ever turned on Siri on your iPhone, it will turn on automatically on your Apple Watch. However, if you need to turn Siri on, here's how to do it.

- Go to setting on your iPhone.
- Go to Siri settings and search.
- Tap the home press switch for Siri on iPhone 8 or later or press the Siri side button on iPhone X or later to turn on Siri for iPhone and Apple Watch.
- Hello Siri

HOW TO TURN OFF AND CHANGE SIRI'S VOICE ON APPLE WATCH

Apple's voice assistant uses your voice to respond to inquiries. As such, it does not require a keyboard or a ton of screen real estate. And because it is context aware, it can handle complex commands and questions. This makes it ideal for something like the Apple Watch, where it can often run faster and more convenient than any other input method.

USE "HEY SIRI" ON YOUR APPLE WATCH

Raise your Apple Watch toward your face (or, if you have disabled the wrist lift, tap the screen to wake up the watch).

Say hi Siri followed by your query.

Note: Hi, Siri will only turn on for the first few seconds of the Apple Watch screen on; If You Can't Make It Work, Remember It!

HOW TO MANUALLY TURN ON SIRI ON YOUR APPLE WATCH

- Hold the digital crown.
- Voice the question or command to Siri.

CHANGE SIRI'S VOICE

But Apple Watch Series 3 and later models offer more verbal pots, which speak to you in response to your questions. This will change your assistant's voice.

- Go to setting on your iPhone
- Navigate to Siri and search.
- Tap sound pots.

- Choose the voice you like.

Note: You may need to connect to Wi-Fi to download more voices.

DISABLE SIRI'S VOICE ON APPLE WATCH

You do not like to listen to Siri on your Apple Watch? This is a quick fix. (Unfortunately, there is no way to change Siri's volume, this is on or off mode).

- Go to the Settings.
- Select pots.
- You can enable or disable it.

FIND YOUR IPHONE WITH YOUR APPLE WATCH

The iPhone is nowhere to be found? Use the Find My iPhone button built into the Apple Watch to find out in no time.

This is a much simpler and less complicated search function.

Note: Your phone must be turned on and Bluetooth enabled for it to work, and it will only plug in the iPhone to which your Apple Watch is paired; Currently can not find other devices this way.

- Press the digital crown button to return to the face of the watch.
- Use your hand to slide up from the watch face. It should display your iPhone at the top as "connected" in green text.
- Tap the Find iPhone button in the lower right corner

In a few seconds, your iPhone should ring with a small submarine-style ping. You can tap this button to your heart's content until you find out where your phone has wasted its time.

HOW TO TURN ON FLIGHT MODE ON APPLE WATCH

With Series 3 and above, Apple introduced LTE in the Apple Watch. While you probably use the feature more on your iPhone than on your Apple Watch, so you can turn on Airplane mode on your Apple Watch ...

- On the clock face, slide up from the control center. Alternatively, you can touch and hold and part of the bottom of an app to access the control center.
- Find the Flight Mode button.
- Tap the flight status icon. It should be orange, indicating that flight mode has now been activated.

When flight mode is on, you will also see an orange plane icon at the top of the clock face. Flight mode turns off mobile radios and Wi-Fi. It will also disable the Bluetooth connection on your iPhone, but will still allow the use of other Bluetooth devices, such as Bluetooth headsets.

CHAPTER TWENTY
CUSTOMIZE THE CLOCK FACE

Customize the face of your Apple Watch to look the way you want and provide the features you need. Choose a design, match colors and features, then add it to your collection. Change face at any time to see the right timing tool or to turn things around.

> ➤ Swipe back and forth across a clock to see other faces in your collection.
> ➤ To see all available clock faces, press and hold the clock face and hold it to the desired one and then tap them.

When you press and hold the clock panel, you see the current clock panel with the share and edit buttons at the bottom. Swipe left or right to see other clock face options. Touch the complication to add the desired functions.

ADD COMPLICATIONS TO THE FACE OF THE WATCH

You can add special features, called complications, to the number of clock faces, so you can instantly check things like stock prices, weather report or information from other apps you have installed.

> ➤ When the clock face is visible, touch and hold the screen, then tap Edit.
> ➤ Slide left to the end.

If the face has complications, they are displayed on the last screen.

> ➤ Touch a complication to select it, then rotate the digital crown to select a new one - activity or pulse, for example.
> ➤ When you are done, click on the digital crown to save your changes and then tap on the face to move to it.

Customization screen for a dashboard with a bold phone complication. Rotate the digital crown to look for complications.

SEE ALL THE FACES OF YOUR WATCH AT A GLANCE.

• Open the Apple Watch app through your iPhone.

- Tap my watch and then slide your collection under my face.
- To rearrange your collection order, tap Edit and drag the reorder icon next to the clock face up or down.

REMOVE FACE FROM YOUR COLLECTION

➢ While the current clock face is displayed, press and hold the screen.

➢ Swipe to the face you do not want, then swipe up and tap Delete.

Alternatively, on your iPhone, open the Apple Watch app, tap my watch and then tap edit in my face area. Tap the Delete button next to the face of the watch you want to delete, then tap Delete.

CHAPTER TWENTY ONE

TIMEKEEPING WITH APPLE WATCH

ADD AND DELETE A CITY

➢ Open the World Clock app.

➢ Touch Add City.

➢ Touch the Dictation, Scribble or Keyboard button and enter the city name.

➢ Touch the city name to add it to the world clock.

To delete a city, swipe left on its name in the list of cities, then press X.

Cities you add to your iPhone also appear on the World Watch on your Apple Watch.

ADD AN ALARM ON YOUR APPLE WATCH

Use the Alarms app to make a sound or vibrate your Apple Watch at a set time.

➢ Open the Alerts app on your Apple Watch.

➢ Touch Add Alarm.

This step is unnecessary when using a 24 hour template.

Two clock screens that show the alarm insertion process: Tap Add Alarm, tap AM or PM, rotate the digital crown to set the time, and then tap Set.

Do not let yourself sleep

SET THE APPLE WATCH AS A BEDSIDE TABLE CLOCK WITH AN ALARM ON APPLE WATCH

- Go to Settings.
- Go to General> Bed Mode and then turn on Bed Mode.

When you connect the Apple Watch to its charger when the nightstand mode is turned on, it displays the current charging status, time and date, and the alarm time you set. To see the time, tap the screen or move your Apple Watch slightly. Even a push or blow on the table can work.

A dark clock is placed on its side and connected to the charger, with the display showing the charging icon in the upper right corner, the current time down and the next alarm time.

If you set an alarm using the Alerts app, the Apple Watch in nightstand mode will gently wake you up with a unique alarm sound.

SET A TIMER ON THE APPLE WATCH

➢ Launch the timer app.

➢ Touch the timer to turn it on.

➢ Scroll down to select last or custom time.

When a timer rings, you can touch back to run a timer of the same length.

CREATE A CUSTOM TIMER

➢ Go to your timer app.

➢ Scroll down and then tap Customize.

➢ Touch hours, minutes or seconds; Rotate the digital crown for adjustment.

Touch Start.

Settings for creating a custom timer, with the time on the left, the minutes in the middle and the seconds on the right. Start and Cancel buttons are below.

Your Apple Watch displays the most recent custom timers under Recent.

HOW TO USE ALARMS, STOPWATCHES AND TIMERS IN APPLE WATCH

Alarms, timers and stopwatches are great tools to take with you.

ALARMS

The Apple Watch allows you to easily set up an alarm, such as a wake-up call at seven in the morning, displayed on an analog or digital screen. To switch between digital and analog, tap the screen and then touch Custom. Swipe left until you see the alarm you like.

> To set up a new alarm on your Apple Watch, follow these steps:
> Click the digital crown button to go to the home screen.
> Tap the alarm app.

This triggers the alarm application

To set the alarm time, turn the Digital Crown knob to adjust the hours and minutes, then tap Set.

Your alarm is already set. You can uncheck the ones you no longer need. You can also long-press the Apple Watch screen in the Alarm app to view options, including alarm snooze (e.g., weekdays). When the alarm sounds, you can touch or cancel later.

You can sync your iPhone alarms with your Apple Watch. This happens automatically by default, but you can also sign in to your Apple Watch app on your iPhone and tap My Clock and then Settings to disable this feature.

Chronometers

You do not have to be an Olympic runner to evaluate a stopwatch that measures the passage of time upwards. Whatever the reason you want to know how much time has passed, the Stopwatch app is what you need, and it is also fully customizable.

That is, the stopwatch app on the Apple Watch allows you to view information in a digital, analog or hybrid view or even a graph showing the real-time average of your lap times.

USE STOPWATCH APP ON APPLE WATCH

follow these steps:

- ➤ Click the digital crown button to go to the home screen.
- ➤ Tap the stopwatch app.
- ➤ This activates the stopwatch application. You can also lift your wrist and then say "Hey Siri, stopwatch" or press and hold the Digital Crown button to activate Siri.
- ➤ Press the green start button in the lower left corner to turn on the stopwatch.

Whether you are in analog, digital or hybrid display, you should see scrolling in time.

Do not worry if you accidentally close the app without paying attention to your time as it is still there when you reopen the app.

Tap the coffee button in the lower right corner of the app if you want to see the graphical averages of coffee times.

Brokers and brokers can evaluate this additional historical information.

SCHEDULE EVENTS WITH STOPWATCH

Schedule events accurately and easily. The Apple Watch can schedule events (up to 11 hours, 55 minutes) and track coffee or split times, then display the results as a list, graph, or live on the clock. The Pro Chronograph and Pro Chronograph watches have the built-in stopwatch.

Start, stop and reset the stopwatch

Open the Stopwatch app on your Apple Watch and do one of the following:

> Home: Press the Green Home button.
> Recorded Coffee: Press the white knee button.
> Input one last time: Press the red stop button.

RESET THE STOPWATCH

- Press the white reset button or the lap key.

Time goes on even if you return to the clock screen or open other apps.

Check the results on the screen you used to measure time or switch screens to analyze your fastest / slowest lap times (circled in green and red) in your preferred format.

If the display includes a list of lap times, rotate the digital crown to scroll.

Analog stopwatch display. Press the right button to start and stop it, and the left button to record knee times.

CHANGE THE STOPWATCH FORMAT

➢ Go to stopwatch app.

➢ Touch the screen to switch between digital, analog, graphic and hybrid formats.

CHAPTER TWENTY TWO

HOW TO READ A MESSAGE ON YOUR APPLE WATCH

Read messages on Apple Watch

Read incoming text messages directly on your Apple Watch, then answer using Dictate, Scribble, or Ready Answer, or go to your iPhone to write a reply.

When you feel a knock or hear an alert tone explaining to you that a message has arrived, lift your Apple Watch to read it.

Rotate the digital crown to scroll to the end of the message.

To jump to the top of the message, touch the top of the screen.

Tip: You can touch a website link within a message to view content in a web format specifically tailored for the Apple Watch. Double-tap to enlarge content.

If the message arrived some time ago, touch and hold the top of the screen, slide the screen down to view the message, and then touch it. To mark the message as read, scroll down and tap Delete. To reject the message without marking the message as read, click Digital Crown.

Message message, with the message icon in the upper right corner and the message below.

See when messages were sent

Touch a conversation in the message list of messages, then swipe left on a message in a conversation.

MUTE OR DELETE A CALL

➢ Mute a call: Swipe left in the call in the message list, then tap the Do Not Disturb button.

➢ Delete call: Swipe left in the call in the call list messages, then tap the trash button.

ACCESS TO PHOTOS, AUDIO AND VIDEO IN THE MESSAGE

Messages can contain pictures, audio, and videos.

➢ **Image:** Touch the image to view it, touch it twice to fill the screen and drag to scroll. When you have

116

finished, tap <in the upper right corner to return to the call.

If you want to save the image, open the message in the messaging app on iPhone and save it there.

Audio clip: tap the clip to listen to it.

The clip is removed after two minutes to save space; If you want to save it, tap Save Under Clip. The audio will stay on for 30 days and you can set it to stay longer on your iPhone: go to settings, tap messages, scroll down to audio messages, tap expire and then tap forever.

Video: Touch the video in the message to start playing the video in full screen. Tap once to display the activation controls. Double-tap to zoom in and rotate the digital crown to adjust the volume. Swipe or press the back button to return to the call.

HOW TO SEND AND REPLY TO MESSAGES ON APPLE WATCH

- Open the messaging app.
- Press and hold the message list until the new message icon appears.

- Tap "New message".
- Tap "Add Contact" to choose.
- Touch the icon to add a contact. (It looks like a silhouette of a person with a plus sign (+) next to it.)
- Select a contact. Then select the phone number or Apple ID you want to use for that person.
- Tap "Create Message".
- Use default replies, emoji, or dictation text to send the message.

Sending a message can be done quickly by tapping the button below the digital crown to open your friends list, where you can select a favorite contact. From there, just tap the message icon to access the messaging options. If you already have a call list available in the Messages app (which you probably do if you use Messages on iPhone), you can also click there to continue the conversation from your wrist.

REPLY TO MESSAGE

How to send messages on Apple Watch Using messages on Apple Watch, you will be notified when you receive an iMessage or a new text message. To read it, simply lift your wrist. You can also view and reply to text messages directly from the messaging application.

- Tap the digital crown to return to your home screen.
- Open the messaging app.
- Choose the one you want.
- Rotate the digital crown to scroll to the end of the message.
- Tap "Reply".
- Use default replies, emoji, or dictation text to send the message.

CUSTOMIZE DEFAULT RESPONSES

How to send messages on the Apple Watch 2 When you reply to a text message on the Apple Watch, Apple offers you half a dozen expressions for an auto-reply, such as "OK" or "Sorry, I can not speak right now." However, these expressions are not exactly personal. For example, I do not think I ever told anyone I could not speak at the moment. You can change the six phrases to make them look a little more like your personality.

- Go to your iphone and open the apple watch app, then.

- Tap my watch.
- Go down.
- Tap "Default Answers".
- Select one of the gray messages, such as "What's wrong?"
- Write your custom message in the text field.

On Apple Watch, when replying to a text message, the custom expressions will appear in the list.

Customize an emoji animation

How to convey a message on the Apple Watch 6 There are three different animated emoji icons on the Apple Watch: a smiley face, a heart and a hand. Each can vary slightly to look different. For example, the smile face can turn into a frown or that the punch can turn into a wave.

In the Reply section of the message, tap the emoji icon.

Swipe left or right to select the emoji you want to use.

When selected, rotate the digital crown to see various animation options, such as a broken heart or a crying face.

If you tap on the animated face or the emoji of the heart, you can change its color.

Click Submit.

SENDING FULL TEXTS BY DICTATING TEXT

Sending messages on Apple Watch 3 To reply to messages that require more than an emoji or saved text reply, you can reply using the Dictate Text feature. It allows you to send longer messages by speaking loudly, which is then sent as an audio message or converted to text. Apple's dictation feature is pretty solid and is a great way to respond quickly to messages.

In the Reply section of the message, tap the microphone icon.

Start talking. Do not forget to include punctuation. For example, if you want to add an exclamation point, say the words "exclamation point".

When finished, tap Finish.

You can choose to send it as an audio clip or text, but if you plan to send it as an audio, you will want to skip the punctuation.

Take some time to experiment with the text-to-speech feature; This will probably be useful for you. With this option plus pre-selected custom responses, you may find yourself sending more and more SMS messages from your wrist instead of pulling out your iPhone.

READ TEXT MESSAGES ON YOUR APPLE WATCH

- Raise your wrist as soon as the message arrives.
- If you do not see the message immediately, swipe down on the dashboard to see your alerts. Unread messages will appear here.
- To view the message you have already opened, click on the digital crown to see all your apps, then touch the message icon (light green with a white chat bubble).
- If Do Not Disturb is turned on, all incoming messages will be muted and you will need to check your iPhone for text messages.

REPLY MESSAGES WITH YOUR APPLE WATCH

When you scroll to the end of the message or thread, you will have several options to answer.

Dictated text message

You can dictate a text response by tapping the microphone icon, speaking into it and writing any punctuation if you wish. Touch the Send button when done.

If you prefer to send audio messages with this feature or would like both options to be available, open the Watch app for iPhone. On the My Clock tab, tap Messaging and then dictate messages and select Transcript (default), Audio or Transcript or Audio.

SUBMIT A CUSTOM RESPONSE USING SCRIBBLE

You can also send a custom reply using Scribble, a function that lets you type across the Apple Watch.

- First, touch the icon with your finger pointing at a dotted line.

123

- Then use your finger to write letters, words, numbers and punctuation that the clock will convert to text.

You can turn the digital crown to edit a letter or select predictive text to complete your word. Touch Send when you have finished writing your message.

SEND A DEFAULT REPLY

Use a default response (such as "OK" or "On the way") by scrolling past the circular icons to see other types of responses. Click the desired reply to send.

You can also create a predefined answer yourself in the Watch iPhone app. Touch the My Clock tab, then Messages and then Default Comments. Touch a default answer to change it, or touch Edit to delete a default answer or change the order in which it appears in the scroll bar.

Reply with tapback

Finally, you can reply with a tapback (online reply to a particular text message) by double-tapping the desired message and selecting your reply (heart, thumbs up, thumbs down, etc.).

SEND NEW TEXT MESSAGE ON APPLE WATCH

- Open the messaging app.
- . Press firmly on the screen until you feel a soft touch, then press New Message.
- Touch Add contact and select from the last contact list that appears, touch the contacts button to view more contacts or touch the keyboard key to enter a phone number.
- Create your message using one of the methods described above, then tap Send when done.

HOW TO DELETE MESSAGES FROM APPLE WATCH

- Click the digital crown on the Apple Watch to activate the home screen of the device.
- Touch the Messages application icon to open your inbox.
- In the conversation you want to delete, swipe left without opening the thread.
- Touch the red trash can icon to delete the thread.

- Touch "Delete" again to confirm that you want to delete the thread. The call will be deleted and removed from your inbox.

CHAPTER TWENTY THREE

DIGITAL TOUCH ON APPLE WATCH

They say a picture is worth a thousand words, so how much do you think touch is worth? With the Apple Watch communication features, you can send tactical response messages to your friends who have Apple Watchs or iPhones with at least iOS 10. So.

HOW TO SEND YOUR HEARTBEAT TO SOMEONE USING APPLE WATCH

When someone gets their heartbeat on their Apple Watch, they get the hefty feedback that will accompany them to something else.

- Open messages from your Apple Watch home screen.
- Select the call to which you want to send a message. Alternatively, force the screen to display the new message option.
- Touch the digital touch button (it looks like two fingers are touching the heart).

- Open the messages, select the desired call and press the digital touch button (it looks like two fingers are touching).
- Hold two fingers on the screen until the heart appears on the screen and begins to beat.
- Remove your fingers from the screen to send. If you are starting a new call, tap the Send button.

CHAPTER TWENTY FOUR

HOW TO USE APPLE PAY ON YOUR APPLE WATCH USING YOUR DEBIT OR CREDIT CARD

You can add multiple cards and change your default card for in-app purchases.

To use Apple Pay, simply double-click the side button and hold the Apple Watch next to a non-contact reader until you feel a light touch.

Apple Watch allows you to do a lot of things without taking out your iPhone (like checking messages, sending quick text responses and turning off iPhone alarms), and using Apple Pay is one of them.

You need to add your card detail first.
- ➢ Open the Clock app for iPhone. Go to the My Clock tab.
- ➢ Touch Wallet and Apple Pay.
- ➢ Touch Add Card and then Next.
- ➢ For cards that have already been added to your iPhone, you will be asked to enter the security code of the card to add it to the Apple Watch. For brand

new cards, you can enter the information via an image by placing your card in a square on the screen or by entering your card details (name, card number, expiration date, security code) manually.

Write down your card details.

➢ After entering your card details, you will be taken to the Terms and Conditions page. Please refer to this page and then tap on which to proceed with the installation process.

➢ Because your card is set up for Apple Pay, "Your bank or card issuer will verify your information and decide if you can use your card with Apple Pay," reads the Apple Support page. "

➢ In the case of my Capital One card, a verification code sent to my iPhone is required. Because I used the iPhone a text message was sent to the code, it was entered automatically and the installation process completed.

A confirmation screen will appear and the card will appear under "Payment cards on your watch".

USE APPLE PAY ON APPLE WATCH

Once you've added cards to your watch, you can use Apple Pay in a number of ways.

- When you are ready to pay at the store that accepts Apple Pay (marked by these icons), double-click the side button. This will pull out your default card.

- Hold your Apple Watch close to the reader without contact, a few inches away, until you feel a light touch.

- To pay with another card, swipe left or right until you reach the card you want to use. Keep the watch close to the reader without contact.

- To change your default card, go to the Wallet and Apple Pay page of the Watch app for iPhone and scroll down to the default transaction section. Touch the default card and select a new default card. You can also enter a default shipping address, email and phone number for automatic completion of future transactions.

HOW TO CHECK YOUR TRANSACTION HISTORY

- Open the Clock app for iPhone. Go to the My Watch tab and tap Wallet and Apple Pay.
- Touch the card for which you want to view transactions, then touch the transactions.

- Make sure the transaction history is turned on. You will see here a list of recent transactions.

Apple payment

Apple payment

- Please note that the amounts you see may be initial authorization amounts, which may be different from the final transaction amount. To see the final transaction amounts, check your credit or debit card statement.

MAKE PURCHASES WITH APPLE WATCH

Pay for in-store purchases through Apple Watch

- Double-click the side button.

- Scroll to select a card.

Hold your Apple Watch a few inches from the non-contact card reader, with the screen facing the reader.

Apple Pay screen with "Hold Near Reader" at the top; Feel a gentle touch and hear a beep when your card details are sent.

Soft touch and beep confirm that payment details have been sent. Receive a message in the message center upon confirmation of the transaction.

On cards that support this, you will also be notified of purchases made with all the cards you added to your wallet, even if you did not add them to your Apple Watch, iPad or iOS device.

You can disable individual notifications and wallet history in your wallet. Just open the Apple Watch app on your iPhone, tap My Watch, go to Wallet and Apple Pay, tap Card, tap Transactions, then turn on or off the View History and enable alerts.

REMOVING CARD FROM APPLE PAY ON YOUR APPLE WATCH

If you receive a new credit or debit card, or your expiration date expires, you will want to remove it from Apple Pay on your Apple Watch.

How to Delete Apple Pay Card on Apple Watch

- On your iphone, enter your apple watch.
- Tap My Clock in the bottom navigation bar if it's not there anymore.
- Touch Passbook and Apple Pay.
- Touch the card you want to delete.
- Touch delete card.
- Tap Delete in the drop-down menu to confirm.

CHAPTER TWENTY FIVE

MAPS AND DIRECTIONS

Find places and explore with Apple Watch

Your Apple Watch has a Maps app to explore your area and get directions.

Ask Siri. Say something like:

"Where am I?"

"Find coffee in me."

SEARCH THE MAP

- Go to maps app
- Tap the Search, click on Dictation, then speak out what you want to do.
- Find service nearby

SEE A GUIDE TO NEARBY ATTRACTIONS AND SERVICES

- Open the Maps application on iPhone, touch the search field, touch the guide and tap Save guide. Then do to your apple watch and launch the Maps app.

- Scroll down, select an editor, and then tap Guide.
- See the iPhone User Guide for information on how to set up and save guides on maps.

VIEW YOUR CURRENT LOCATION AND ENVIRONMENT

- You can view it by Opening your Maps app
- Touch location.

Maps application that displays a map. Your location is shown as a blue dot on the map. There is a blue fan above the position point, indicating that the clock is facing north.

Move and zoom

Panorama from the map: Drag with one finger.

Zoom in or out on the map: Rotate the digital crown.

You can also double-tap the map to get closer to where you tap.

Return to your current location: Tap the location button in the lower right corner.

Get information about a landmark or a marked location

Touch the location marker on the map.

Rotate the digital crown to scroll through the information.

Touch <in the upper right corner to return to the map.

Tip: To call the location, enter the phone number in the location information. To switch to your iPhone, open the App Switcher. (On an iPhone with Face ID, slide up from the bottom edge and pause; on an iPhone with the Home button, double-click the Home button). Touch the button at the bottom of the screen to unlock the phone.

DROP, MOVE AND DELETE MAP MARKERS

Position a cursor: Click and hold the map where you want the cursor to go, wait for the drop and then release it.

> ➢ Move Cursor: Release a new cursor in the new location.
> ➢ Delete Pin: Touch it to view the address information, rotate the digital crown to scroll, and then touch the Delete icon.

The Maps app displays a map with a purple pin placed on it, through which you can get the approximate address of a place on the map or as a destination for directions.

Tip: To find the approximate address of any place on the map, place a pin on the location and then touch the cursor to view the address information.

VIEW A CONTACT'S ADDRESS ON THE MAP

➢ Open the Maps app on your Apple Watch.
➢ Touch Search and then touch the Contacts button.
➢ Rotate the digital crown to scroll and then touch the direction.
➢ Scroll down, then tap the map.

FIND A ROUTE

CarPlay generates possible destinations using addresses from your email, text messages, contacts and calendars, as well as the places you visit. You can also search for locations, use locations you have saved as favorites and collections, and find attractions and services nearby.

Ask Siri. Say something like:

"Find a gas station""Give me directions to get home"

"Take me to the Golden Gate Bridge"

"Find a charging station"

"Find coffee in my hands"

Alternatively, you can use the controls built into your vehicle to open maps in CarPlay and select a route.

Note: If you are viewing the CarPlay Dashboard and maps do not appear in the list of recent applications on the left, tap the home button to see the pages of all your CarPlay apps, including Maps.

When maps are open in CarPlay, do one of the following:

➢ Choose a place you have saved as a favorite. (See Save favorite places on maps on iPhone.)
➢ Select destinations and then select a last destination or scroll to select a destination you have saved in the collection. (See Organizing Places in My Guides on Maps on iPhone).
➢ Select Search, then select the microphone button to talk about a search phrase, or select the keyboard button to use the on-screen keyboard (if available).

You can also select a destination from a nearby service category, such as parking or restaurants.

➤ If multiple routes appear, use your vehicle controls to select your preferred route.

To call the destination before leaving, select the phone button.

To start getting directions by rotation, select Go.

Maps show directions from your current location.

When you get to your destination and get out of your car, a parked car marker will appear on the maps on the iPhone so you can find your way back to your car.

HOW TO USE APPLE WATCH FOR INSTRUCTIONS

➤ Touch the location on the map to open the information screen and touch the Instructions button.

➤ Release a pin and then tap it to bring up the information screen and press the instruction button.

- ➤ Ask for remover instructions. The Virtual Assistant will automatically open Apple Maps with out-of-the-box instructions.
- ➤ Tap the screen and look for an address from your contacts or use the dictation feature to search for a business or landmark.

Get started working with Apple Maps on your iPhone. The app will sync automatically with the Apple Watch. Once you have entered the information in the iPhone app, open the Clock app for instructions.

CHAPTER TWENTY SIX

MUSIC ON APPLE WATCH

How to control music on iPhone using Apple Watch

- ➢ Raise your wrist to turn on your Apple Watch and the watch face will appear.
- ➢ Click on a digital crown and the home screen will appear.
- ➢ Touch music and the music application will open. If the music application displays a screen other than the music screen, tap the button in the upper right corner once or more to display the music screen.
- ➢ Touch a strong screen and the options screen will appear.
- ➢ Touch the font to open the font screen.
- ➢ Touch the iPhone and the music screen will appear again.
- ➢ Touch the view you want to use: artists, albums, songs, playlists.

When the screen appears, touch the artist, album, song, or playlist you want to listen to. If you touch the album, for example, the songs on the album will appear.

You can rotate the digital crown to scroll up or down the list. Note that the music app only shows the album songs that are on your iPhone. Therefore, the list you see on your Apple Watch may not be complete.

Touch the song you want to play first and the song will start playing. (You can touch the previous to return to the beginning of the current song or touch the previous again to return to the beginning of the previous song.

A few words about listening to music with the Apple Watch

Of course users can use their Apple Watch to listen to music on their iPhones, but they can also sync a playlist to enjoy the music on their Apple Watch without using their iPhone. Users can play music on their Apple Watch without their iPhone if they can be paired with Bluetooth headsets. To do this:

MAKE A PLAYLIST FOR MUSIC

Note that you can keep a music playlist at any time on your Apple Watch. Also note that audiobooks and podcasts are not supported:

- Launch the music app.

- Touch the Library tab.

- Touch Playlists> New Playlist.

- Choose a name for your playlist.

- Search for albums you want to add.

- When you find a song or other item you want to add, tap add.

- After adding the item, tap Finish (you can continue to search for more music to add).

- When you have finished adding music, touch Finish to save the playlist you have created.

HOW TO SYNC THE PLAYLIST

Before proceeding, place the Apple Watch on its charger and make sure the watch is charged.

- Enter Settings tap Bluetooth and turn it on, in your iPhone.

- Tap My Watch tab From the Apple Watch app on your iPhone,.

- Touch Music> Synced Music.

- Now tap the playlist you want to sync with your Apple Watch.

When a message next to your playlist says pending sync, your playlist will start syncing from your iPhone to your Apple Watch. Please wait until the synchronization is complete before using the watch. Can ab Launch the Apple Watch app on your iPhone and tap Music if you want to see the sync progress.

Note that you may need to download any music stored in the cloud, such as music from Apple Music or iTunes Match, to your iPhone before you can sync it to your Apple Watch.

HOW TO LISTEN TO A PLAYLIST ON APPLE WATCH

Note that you cannot listen to your playlist on your Apple Watch until you pair your smartwatch with a Bluetooth headset. After adjusting, continue as follows:

- On your Apple Watch, tap the Music app on the Home screen.
- Tap the screen and tap Source> Apple Watch.
- Then tap Playlists.

SHUFFLE OR REPEAT MUSIC

Mix albums, songs and artists from the music screen: Touch an album, artist or playlist, then touch the shuffle button.

Shuffle or repeat music from the play screen: While watching the play screen, press the queue button and then press the shuffle button or the play button.

Touch Repeat twice to repeat a song.

SEE HOW MUCH MUSIC IS STORED ON THE APPLE WATCH

➢ Open the Settings app on your Apple Watch.

➢ Go to General> Usage.

DELETE MUSIC FROM APPLE WATCH

➢ Unlock your iPhone and tap the apple watch app.

➢ Tap my watch and then music.

➢ Turn off automatically added playlists that you do not want on your Apple Watch.

➢ To delete other music you have added to your Apple Watch, tap Edit, then tap the Delete button next to Junk.

HOW TO PAIR BLUETOOTH HEADSET ON APPLE WATCH

➤ go to Settings, then enter Bluetooth on your apple watch.

➤ Turn on the headphones and turn on pairing mode. It varies from ear to ear, most of them will hold the power button pressed for a few seconds, while others (like AirPods) will have a dedicated adjustment button that will be pressed for a few seconds.

Wait until you see your Bluetooth headset on your Apple Watch, tap the Bluetooth device to pair.

Wait a few seconds for the Apple Watch to match your Bluetooth headset.

If you succeed, you will see "connected" next to your Bluetooth device.

CHAPTER TWENTY SEVEN

PHOTO ON APPLE WATCH

In Apple Watch, browse your photos in the Photos app and show a photo across the clock.

The main screen of the Photos app on Apple Watch, with a number of photos displayed on the web.

VIEW PHOTO MEMORY ON APPLE WATCH

View last memory above Siri Clock: Select Siri Clock, then tap Memory.

See photos from "Memories" across the clock: Open the Apple Watch app on your iPhone, tap the face gallery, tap the face of photos and then tap dynamic.

The Dynamic Clock Panel displays pictures of your recent memories and updates when you have new ones.

LIMIT IMAGE STORAGE ON THE APPLE WATCH

The number of photos stored on your Apple Watch depends on the availability. To save space for songs or other content, you can limit the number of images stored in it.

- Unlock your iPhone and enter the apple watch app.
- Tap My Clock and then go to Photos> Photo Limit.

TO SEE HOW MANY PHOTOS ARE IN YOUR APPLE WATCH

- Go to Settings
- Tap General
- Launch the Apple Watch
- Click Watch and then General> About.

To see how much space is used for your photos, go to General> Using the Apple Watch app.

TAKE A SCREENSHOT OF THE APPLE WATCH

- Open the Settings app on your Apple Watch, go to General, then Run Play Screenshots.
- Simultaneously press the digital crown and side button to capture the screen.

www.ingramcontent.com/pod-product-compliance
Lightning Source LLC
La Vergne TN
LVHW051340050326
832903LV00031B/3654